Little Koala Adopts a Puppy

A LESSON ON THE IMPORTANCE OF PET CARE RESPONSIBILITIES

THE LIFE SKILLS SERIES: BOOK # 5

Copyright © 2026 by Amanda Aliff, LPC, NCC, CCTP

All rights reserved. No part of this book may be reproduced or transmitted in any form or by any means, electronic or mechanical, including photocopying, recording, or by any information storage and retrieval system, without written permission in writing from the copyright owner. This book was printed in the United States of America.

ISBN-13 (PAPERBACK): 978-1-961752-76-4
ISBN-13 (HARDCOVER): 978-1-961752-77-1

Available on Amazon and other retail outlets.

This book series is designed to teach children important skills.

Each book in the series has a different theme related to life skills. A separate section in the back provides important topics covered throughout the book in addition to follow up questions for families to ask their children. The questions are meant to create open communication and further conversation regarding important life lessons.

This book series is recommended for children between the ages of four through nine, but could be used for children of all ages.

This book is dedicated to all dog lovers.

Come along on a journey and learn with Little Koala!

Along the way you will see a lot of dog bones!

How many dog bones can you find?

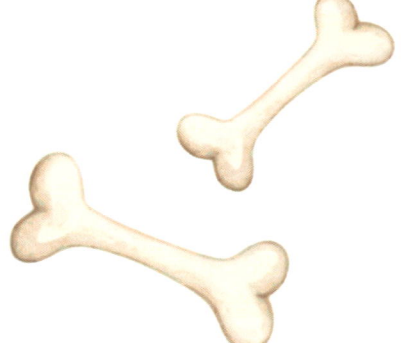

Today is the day. Little Koala has been waiting all week for this moment.

The family is taking a trip to the animal shelter so that Little Koala can pick out his very own puppy.

During the drive, Mama Koala gently reminds him, "you know that taking care of a puppy is a lot of responsibility."

Little Koala thinks of all the things that Mama Koala told him leading up to this moment.

How he will need to feed the puppy, walk the puppy, take the puppy outside, and teach the puppy.

Little Koala's thoughts are interrupted because...

THEY HAVE ARRIVED!

Little Koala immediately notices one little puppy sitting in the corner and says, "that's the one!"

"I am going to name him Duke," Little Koala proudly announces.

Little Koala gets home and plays with Duke for hours.

Little Koala quickly learns...

Duke likes to chew on shoes.

Duke cries at night when he feels lonely.

Sometimes Duke goes potty inside the house.

Duke has very sharp teeth and likes to nibble on Little Koala's fingers.

Duke does not listen very well.

Little Koala feels exhausted.

He did not know that adopting Duke would be so much work.

Mama Koala notices that Little Koala looks exhausted and gently tells him, "There are a few important things to remember when caring for a new puppy."

1. Puppies are new to the world and learning, so they require patience.

2. Taking care of a puppy is a big responsibility because your puppy depends on you to take care of all their needs.

3. Just like the puppy needs to learn how to be with humans, it is just as important for the family to learn how to be with the puppy.

Mama Koala reminds Little Koala that training will be a lot of work and will take patience...

...but the love that Duke will give him makes it all worth it.

"I am always here to help you when you need it, Little Koala," says Mama.

"I know, Mama," says Little Koala, "now let us go train that puppy!"

Do you know what kinds of things you need to do to take care of a puppy?

Talking points for parents:

- Needs versus wants.
- The importance of communication.
- The responsibilities of caring for a pet.
- Different ways that beings communicate (i.e. dogs will whine or bark to communicate).
- The importance of patience.
- Discussing situations where patience is necessary.

Questions to ask your child:

1. What is a responsibility?
2. Why are responsibilities important?
3. What responsibilities do you have now?
4. What responsibilities go into taking care of a pet?
5. What helps you remember your responsibilities?
6. Why is communication important?
7. What does "exhausted" feel like?
8. Can you think of a situation you experienced where you felt exhausted?
9. Why is it important to ask for help?
10. Can you think of a time that you asked someone else for help?

Meet the Author:

Amanda Aliff is a Licensed Professional Counselor and the owner of Aliff Counseling Services, LLC.

She is deeply passionate about nurturing emotional growth and resilience in young minds and is on a mission to teach essential life skills through creative, engaging, and developmentally meaningful storytelling.

This book series was a true family effort; her husband and their three children all played meaningful roles in bringing these stories to life.

Check out the entire Little Koala Life Skills Collection!

Can you lead Duke to his bone?

www.ingramcontent.com/pod-product-compliance
Lightning Source LLC
LaVergne TN
LVRC092314110526
838202LV00107B/2623